Made in United States
North Haven, CT
18 March 2023

34245583R00070